INTRODUCTION

Just as for us today she stands apart in her unique atmosphere and architecture, in the Renaissance and the Baroque Venice stood apart as a centre of religious music. In Rome, Milan and Bologna, Italy's other main musical centres, such activity was dominated by the principal churches or cathedrals; but in Venice it was the basilica of S. Marco, private chapel of the temporal rulers, the Doges, which set the standards of excellence (the cathedral church was in fact on an island at the eastern edge of the city). Though the sixteenth and seventeenth centuries witnessed a decline in the political and economic power of the great Venetian empire, the strong libertarian spirit and wonderful flowering of culture in its capital city was more than ample compensation. Venice was still a great mercantile centre, of course, and the hub of the music printing industry in its first centuries of existence, so that many composers found their way there to oversee publication of their music, and would have been able to witness the glories of Venetian ceremonial music at first hand.

Because services in S. Marco were held at the behest of the civil rather than the spiritual power, Venetian festivities represented a unique fusion of civic and the ecclesiastical, and the people of the city were involved to a degree unparalleled elsewhere. Not only did the basilica have its own liturgy (the St Mark's use, a 'dialect' of the widely-used Roman rite that had its origins in antiquity), but the ceremonial books prescribed very precisely what sort of music was to be performed on various types of feast. The ecclesiastical calendar gave special importance not only to feasts like Christmas, Easter and St Mark's Day, but also to various saints whose days coincided with anniversaries of great events in Venetian history. The apotheosis of such church-state festivity was the famous *Bucintoro* or 'marriage to the sea' ceremony held every year on the Vigil of Ascension Day, when the Doge and his retinue were rowed out into the lagoon in magnificent barges and the Doge cast a ring into the water to symbolize Venice's maritime power.

Occasions such as this are recorded in many well-known Venetian paintings, as are the noble religious processions in the Piazza S. Marco. Sometimes these latter marked very solemn occasions, such as that in 1618 when a fragment of the true cross was brought to Venice and carried in procession; it is thought that Monteverdi's motet *Christe adoramus te* (which ends this volume) was written for this event.

Some of the best-known Venetian ceremonial music was, of course conceived on a grand scale for the mixed vocal and instrumental ensemble that made up the musical establishment at S. Marco. The first instrumentalists had been engaged for the choir in 1568, and by Giovanni Gabrieli's time as organist (1585-1612), music requiring several choirs and many instruments was the order of the day on many great feasts. The younger Gabrieli is absent from the present collection simply because he wrote scarcely anything for fewer than eight voices; fortunately his uncle Andrea Gabrieli, who has been unjustifiably overshadowed by Giovanni, did write plenty of straightforward music for the church year, and can be generously represented here. The glittering special occasions, however, were not the only services for which music was required at S. Marco. Moreover the published Venetian motet books were clearly aimed at the generality of ordinary churches all over the Venetian Republic, which covered much of northern Italy.

There were in any case several other churches in Venice itself which had a flourishing, if less splendid and widely renowned, musical life. They included the Dominican church of SS. Giovanni e Paulo, the Augustinian church of S. Stefano (where G. Gabrieli is buried), and the Franciscan church of the Frari (where Monteverdi is buried). These fine, lofty Gothic buildings are very different from the Byzantine richness of S. Marco; their music is represented in this volume by the motet by the priest Giacomo Finetti, who was organist at the Frari from 1613 till his death in the terrible Venetian plague of 1631. Finetti's motets were exceptionally popular not only in Italy but also north of the Alps, in Germany. And then there were the Venetian *scuole grandi*, or confraternities, which organized music to celebrate their patronal days, often hiring musicians from S. Marco and elsewhere in the city. There is a famous description by an English traveller, Thomas Coryat, of the celebrations for the feast of S. Rocco at the *scuola* of that saint in 1608, which included a Vespers lasting several hours with wonderful music. Giovanni Gabrieli played the organ on this occasion and indeed seems to have been regularly employed by this institution as well as at S. Marco. For many smaller Venetian churches unable to support any permanent musical establishment, musicians from S. Marco would provide a choir for a special occasion, so that at least the patronal festival could be marked by fine music.

Apart from Finetti, just mentioned, all the composers represented in this volume were employed at S. Marco in some capacity. Willaert, who was maestro there from 1527 till his death in 1562, did much to put Venetian music on the map, developing the polychoral style often associated with the basilica and attracting a distinguished circle of pupils. He went there at a time when Flemings were still going south to Italy and his music therefore represents the classic Franco-Flemish contrapuntal style at its height. Andrea Gabrieli was second organist from 1564 to 1584, having worked previously at S. Geremia, one of the smaller Venetian churches. Well-known for madrigals and instrumental music, he wrote motets with a lightness of touch that is most attractive. The three included here are from his two collections covering the whole church year and aimed at the ordinary church choir. Claudio Merulo was almost an exact contemporary of Andrea, and was first organist of the basilica in the same years that Andrea held the second position; his Easter motet comes from a collection similar in aim to Andrea's, providing festive music for the church year, though this time in a more solid manner. Giovanni Croce, who came from Chioggia (the 'mini-Venice' at the southern end of the lagoon) had a long career at S. Marco as boy singer, priest, vice-maestro and finally maestro from 1603 until his death in 1609. *Beati eritis* comes from his most popular publication, of fluent and simple four-part music for less well-found choirs. Lastly we have the great Monteverdi, who became maestro in 1613 (next but one after Croce) and built up the choir afresh after a rather thin period in the first decade of the seventeenth century. Very few of his motets are choral in the traditional way, but *Christe adoramus te* is one exception, combining rich chromatic harmonies and the dignified tread of what by now was consciously known as the *stile antico* - the 'old style'.

Sources

Source details are given at the top of each piece. In view of the practical nature of the volume, one appropriate, reliable source for each piece has been selected, and therefore no cross-references are made to alternative readings.

Willaert, *Pater noster - Ave Maria*: the source cited is not the earliest for this paired motet, but it is arguably closest to the composer; it shows all the accidentals that create sometimes surprising harmonies. A. Gabrieli, *O Rex gloriae*, S.69-76 (1565): there appears to be two bars' music too much; the passage is emended in line with the Venice reprint of 1572.

Editorial method

Note values have generally been halved, and quartered in triple-time passages. Prefatory staves indicate original clefs, pitch and mensuration. Ditto marks in word underlay have been expanded without notice. Editorial accidentals are placed above the notes to which they apply. ⌐──┐ and ⌐ ¬ are used to indicate ligatures and coloration respectively in the source. Modern voice designations are editorial. All other editorial additions are placed in square brackets. The organ parts in the Willaert and the first of the Andrea Gabrieli pieces are reductions which may be used in performance as well as rehearsal; in the later two Andrea Gabrieli, the Merula and Croce pieces they are realizations of the *basso seguente* used to provide an improvised accompaniment in the period leading up to the introduction of the *basso continuo*.

Jerome Roche

Meisterwerke aus Venedig

EINLEITUNG

Die Stadt Venedig, die uns heute vor allem durch ihre besondere Atmosphäre und Architektur besticht, war während der Renaissance und des Barock in vergleichbarem Maße als ein Zentrum der Kirchenmusik ausgezeichnet. Die musikalischen Aktivitäten in Rom, Mailand und Bologna, Italiens anderen Musikzentren, wurden durch die großen Kirchen oder Kathedralen beherrscht. In Venedig dagegen wurden die künstlerischen Maßstäbe durch die private Kapelle der weltlichen Herrscher, der Dogen, gesetzt, nämlich an der Basilika von S. Marco; die eigentliche Kathedral-Kirche befand sich bezeichnenderweise auf einer Insel am östlichen Rand der Stadt. Der in Venedig herrschende freiheitsliebende Geist und die blühende Kultur der Stadt bildeten im sechzehnten und siebzehnten Jahrhundert mehr als nur einen Ausgleich zu dem politischen und wirtschaftlichen Niedergang der Venezianischen Republik. Venedig war natürlich nach wie vor ein großes Wirtschaftszentrum und Mittelpunkt der Druckindustrie im ersten Jahrhundert des Bestehens dieses Wirtschaftszweiges, so daß viele Komponisten zur Drucklegung ihrer Werke in die Stadt kamen und dabei Gelegenheit hatten, den Prunk venezianischer Festmusiken an Ort und Stelle mitzuerleben.

Da die Gottesdienste in S. Marco eher auf Geheiß weltlicher denn geistlicher Herrscher abgehalten wurden, stellten Feierlichkeiten in Venedig eine ganz einzigartige Mischung bürgerlicher Kultur und kirchlicher Riten dar; die Bevölkerung Venedigs war auf eine Weise bei der Gestaltung der Feierlichkeiten eingebunden, die man nirgendwo sonst kannte. An der Basilika von S. Marco gab es nicht nur eine eigene Liturgie – praktisch eine Nebenform des römischen Ritus, der seinerseits auf antike Vorformen zurückgeht –, sondern auch sehr präzise Vorschriften, welche Musik zu welchen Kirchenfesten aufgeführt wurde. Der Kirchenkalender wies nicht nur Feste wie Weihnachten, Ostern und den Tag des Namenspatrons Markus als besondere Feiertage aus, sondern auch die Festtage verschiedener Kirchenheiliger, die mit Jahrestagen von Ereignissen stadtgeschichtlicher Bedeutung zusammenfielen. Der Höhepunkt solcher städtischer Festtage war die berühmte *Bucintoro*-Feier (Vermählung mit dem Meer), die jedes Jahr am Vorabend von Himmelfahrt darin bestand, daß der Doge mit seinem Gefolge in prunkvollen Barken auf die Lagune gerudert wurde, um dann einen Ring ins Wasser zu werfen, der die maritime Macht Venedigs demonstrieren sollte.

Viele bekannte Abbildungen Venedigs dokumentieren Ereignisse wie das eben beschriebene, aber auch die feierlichen religiösen Prozessionen auf dem Markusplatz. Solche Prozessionen konnten durch sehr erhabene Ereignisse veranlaßt sein, wie etwa eine Prozession im Jahr 1618, als ein Teil des Kreuzes Jesu nach Venedig gebracht und in einer Prozession zur Kirche getragen wurde. Man nimmt an, daß Monteverdis Motette *Christe adoramus te*, die am Ende unserer Sammlung steht, zu diesem Anlaß geschrieben wurde.

Zu den heute bekanntesten Festmusiken Venedigs gehören die groß angelegten Stücke, die für das gemischte vokale und instrumentale Ensemble von S. Marco geschrieben wurden. Im Jahr 1568 waren die ersten Instrumentalisten für die Kapelle engagiert worden, und als Giovanni Gabrieli Organist war (1585-1612), gehörte die Aufführung mehrchöriger Musik mit vielen Instrumenten anläßlich zahlreicher großer Feste praktisch zur Tagesordnung. Der jüngere Gabrieli ist in der vorliegenden Sammlung nicht vertreten, weil er praktisch nichts für eine Besetzung mit weniger als acht Stimmen hinterlassen hat; glücklicherweise hat sein Onkel Andrea Gabrieli, der durch das Werk Giovannis leider in zu starkem Maße in den Hintergrund gedrängt wird, zahlreiche kirchenmusikalische Werke für das Kirchenjahr geschrieben und ist in unserer Ausgabe gut vertreten. Die herausragenden Festgottesdienste zu besonderen Anlässen waren allerdings nicht die einzigen Gottesdienste, für die in S. Marco Kompositionen benötigt wurden. Und die gedruckten Sammlungen mit Motetten aus Venedig waren darüberhinaus eindeutig für den Gottesdienst in den schlichten Kirchen der Venezianischen Republik gedacht, die sich über den Großteil Norditaliens erstreckte.

In Venedig selber gab es neben S. Marco noch andere Kirchen, die ein starkes musikalisches Eigengewicht hatten, wenn auch vielleicht etwas weniger großartig und weniger bekannt. Dazu gehören die Dominikanerkirche SS. Giovanni e Paulo, die Augustinerkirche S. Stefano (G. Gabrieli ist dort beigesetzt) und die Franziskanerkirche S. Maria dei Frari (Beisetzungsstätte von Monteverdi). Diese schönen, erlesenen gotischen Gebäude unterscheiden sich stark von der byzantinischen Pracht an S. Marco. Die Musik dieser Kirchen wird in unserer Sammlung durch die Motette des Priesters Giacomo Finetti vertreten, der von 1613 bis zu seinem Tod während des großen Pestjahres in Venedig 1631 als Organist an S. Maria dei Frari wirkte. Finettis Motetten waren nicht nur in Italien, sondern auch nördlich der Alpen in Deutschland außerordentlich bekannt.

In Venedig gab es neben den Kirchen außerdem noch die *scuole grandi* oder Brüderschaften, die zur Feier ihrer Patronatstage musikalische Ereignisse organisierten, oft indem sie Musiker von S. Marco oder anderswo aus der Stadt dazu heranzogen. Der englische Reisende, Thomas Coryat, hat eine berühmte Beschreibung der Feierlichkeiten zum Fest von S. Rocco in der *scuola* dieses Heiligen im Jahr 1608 hinterlassen, die unter anderem aus einer sich über mehrere Stunden hinziehenden Vesper mit Musik bestand. Musiker von S. Marco wurden von kleineren Kirchen Venedigs verpflichtet, die sich eine ständigen Kapelle nicht leisten konnten, so daß dort zumindest die Patronatstage durch gute Musik ausgezeichnet werden konnten.

Abgesehen von dem eben erwähnten Finetti, waren alle in unserer Sammlung vertretenen Komponisten in irgend-einer Funktion an S. Marco tätig. Willaert, der dort von 1527 bis zu seinem Tod im Jahr 1562 Kapellmeister war, trug viel dazu bei, Venedig einen bleibenden Platz in der Musikgeschichte zu sichern. So entwickelte er den mehrchörigen Stil, der mit der Basilika in Zusammenhang gebracht wird, und versammelte einen großen Kreis hervorragender Schüler um sich. Willaert kam nach Venedig, als die Flamen noch gen Süden nach Italien zogen, so daß seine Werke den klassischen Stil franko-flämischen Kontrapunkts in seinem Höhepunkt repräsentieren. Andrea Gabrieli war von 1564 bis 1584 zweiter Organist, nachdem er vorher an S. Geremia, einer der kleineren Kirchen Venedig gewirkt hatte. Er ist bekannt für seine Madrigale und Instrumentalmusik, schrieb aber auch wegen ihrer klanglichen Durchsichtigkeit äußerst reizvolle Motetten. Die drei von ihm hier vorgestellten Motetten stammen aus seinen beiden Sammlungen mit Motetten durch das Kirchenjahr, die für einen schlichten Chor bestimmt waren. Claudio Merulo ist ein Zeitgenosse von Andrea Gabrieli; er war zu der Zeit erster Organist an der Basilika von S. Marco, als A. Gabrieli das Amt des zweiten Organisten ausfüllte. Merulos Ostermotette stammt aus einer Sammlung, die wie die Sammlungen Gabrielis festliche Musik für das Kirchenjahr anbietet, allerdings etwas einfacher im Stil. Giovanni Croce kam aus Chioggia, dem verkleinerten Abbild Venedigs am südlichen Ende der Lagune, und hatte eine lange Wirkungszeit an S. Marco als Chorknabe, Priester, Vize-Kapellmeister und schließlich Kapellmeister von 1603 bis zu seinem Tod 1609. *Beati eritis* stammt aus seiner bekanntesten Sammlung mit flüssig geschriebenen und einfachen vierstimmigen Werken für weniger gut ausgestattete Chöre. Schließlich haben wir ein Werk des großen Monteverdi, der 1613 Kapellmeister wurde (als übernächster Chorleiter nach Croce), und den Chor nach einer relativ schwachen Periode im ersten Jahrzehnt des siebzehnten Jahrhunderts neu aufbaute. Nur wenige seiner Motetten sind im traditionellen chorischen Stil gehalten, aber das von uns vorgestellte *Christe adoramus te* ist eine der wenigen Ausnahmen und vereint reiche chromatische Harmonien mit ehrwürdigen Stilmerkmalen des nun als *stile antico* bewußt komponierten 'alten Stiles'.

Quellen

Angaben zu den Quellen werden über jedem einzelnen Werk mitgeteilt. Angesichts der Tatsache, daß es sich hier um eine Ausgabe für die musikalische Praxis handelt, wurde jeweils eine sinnvolle, verläßliche Quelle für jedes Werk ausgesucht; auf Verweise zu anderen, abweichenden Lesarten wurde verzichtet.

Die Quelle zu dem *Pater noster - Ave Maria* von Willaert ist nicht die früheste Quelle für diese Doppelmotette; dennoch wird diese Quelle allen anderen vorgezogen, da sie wohl in engster Verbindung zum Komponisten steht. Die genannte Quelle weist sämtliche Versetzungszeichen auf, die zu den manchmal überraschenden Harmonien führen. In der Quelle zu A. Gabrieli, *O Rex gloriae*, gibt es auf S. 69-76 in der Ausgabe von 1565 zwei offensichtlich überzählige Takte. Diese beiden Takte wurden in Übereinstimmung mit dem venezinianischen Nachdruck von 1572 emendiert.

Zur Edition

Die Werke wurden generell unter Verkürzung der Notenwerte auf die Hälfte, bei dreizeitigen Abschnitten unter Verkürzung der Notenwerte auf ein Viertel übertragen. Die vorangestellten Notensysteme geben die ursprüngliche Schlüsselung, Tonhöhe und Mensur wieder. Textwiederholungen der Quelle, die mit einem *idem*-Zeichen notiert sind, wurden ohne entsprechenden Hinweis ausgeschrieben. Vom Herausgeber zugesetzte Akzidentien werden über die Noten gesetzt, für die sie gelten.⌐‾ und ⌐ ‾ werden benutzt, um auf Ligatur bzw. Kolorierung in der Quelle hinzuweisen. Die modernen Stimmbezeichnungen stammen vom Herausgeber. Alle anderen herausgeberischen Ergänzungen werden durch eckige Klammern gekennzeichnet. Die Orgel-Stimme in der Willaert-Motette und in der ersten der beiden Motetten von Andrea Gabrieli sind Klavierauszüge, die sowohl bei der Probe als auch bei der Aufführung gespielt werden können. Bei den beiden anderen Motetten von Andrea Gabrieli, dem Werk von Merula und der Motette von Croce handelt es sich um einen ausgesetzten *basso seguente*, der in der Zeit vor der Einführung des *basso continuo* eine improvisierte Begleitung ermöglichte.

Jerome Roche

*Pater noster – Ave Maria

Musica quatuor vocum … liber secundus
(Venice, Gardano, 1545)

Adrian Willaert
(*c.*1490–1562)

*Both *Pater noster* and *Ave Maria* may be performed separately.
'Pater noster' und 'Ave Maria' können auch einzeln aufgeführt werden.

© 1994 by Faber Music Ltd.
This music is copyright. Photocopying is illegal.

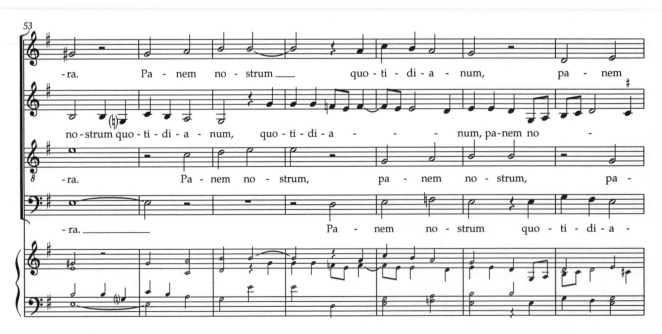

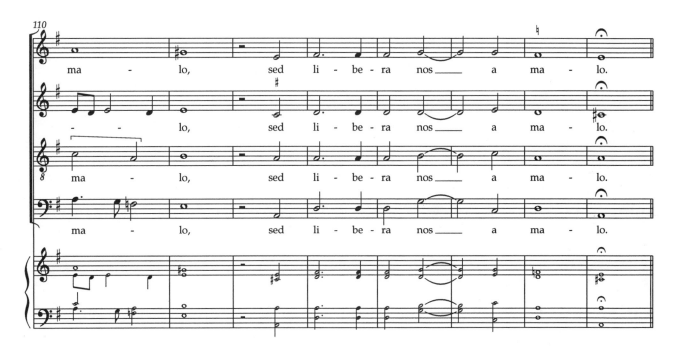

SECUNDA PARS [Ave Maria]

14

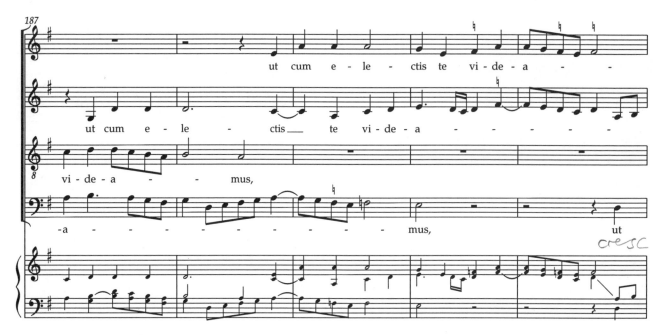

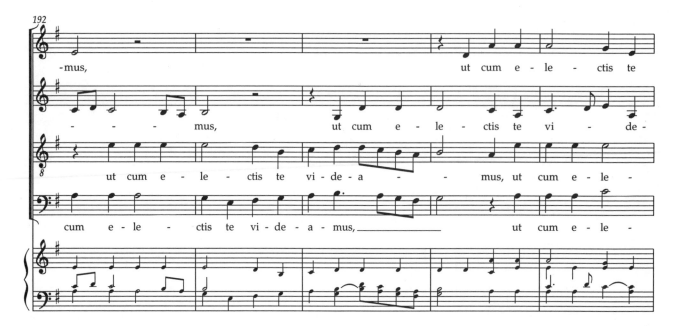

O Rex gloriae

Sacrae cantiones quinque vocum … liber primus
(Venice, Gardano, 1565)

Andrea Gabrieli
(*c*.1510-1586)

Angelus ad pastores ait

Ecclesiasticarum cantionum quatuor vocum… liber primus
(Venice, Gardano, 1576)

Andrea Gabrieli
(*c.*1510-1586)

Hodie completi sunt

Ecclesiasticarum cantionum quatuor vocum … liber primus
(Venice, Gardano, 1576)

Andrea Gabrieli
(*c.*1510-1586)

-di - de-rit et bap - ti - za - tus fu - e - rit,

et bap - ti - za-tus fu - - e - rit, sal - vus

qui __ cre - di - de-rit et bap - ti - za - tus fu - - e -

-di - de-rit et bap - ti - za-tus fu - - e -

sal - vus e - rit, sal - vus e - rit, al - le - lu - ia, al - le - lu -

e - rit, __ sal - vus e - rit, al - le - lu - ia, al - le - lu - ia,

-rit, sal - vus e - rit, al - le - lu - ia, al - le - lu -

-rit, sal - vus e - rit, al - le - lu - ia, al - le - lu -

-ia, al - le - - lu - ia, al - le - - lu - ia.

al - le - - lu - ia, al - le - lu - ia.

-ia, al - le - - lu - ia, al - le - - lu - ia.

-ia, al - le - - lu - ia.

Haec est dies

Liber primus sacrarum cantionum quinque vocibus
(Venice, Gardano, 1578)

Claudio Merulo
(1533-1604)

Beati eritis

Motetti a quattro voci … libro primo
(Venice, Vincenti, 1597)

Giovanni Croce
(c.1557-1609)

* A in source / *A in der Quelle*

O crux ave spes unica

Corona Mariae quatuor concinenda … liber quintus
(Venice, Magni, 1622)

Giacomo Finetti
(*fl.* 1605-31)

* # on 3rd, not 2nd note of bar in source/*In der Quelle steht das # nicht auf der zweiten, sondern auf der dritten Note des Taktes.*

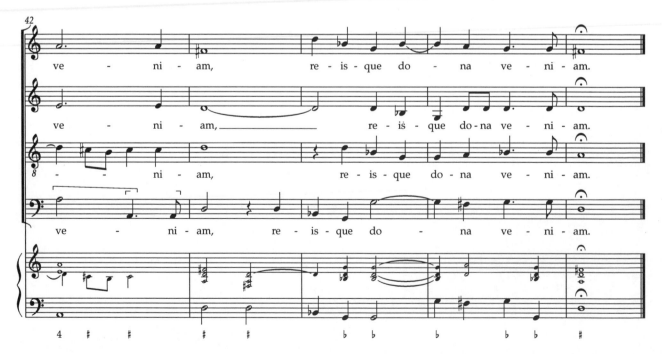

Translations

Pater noster - Ave Maria

Our Father, who art in heaven, hallowed be thy name. Thy kingdom come. Thy will be done on earth, as it is in heaven. Give us this day our daily bread. And forgive us our trespasses, as we forgive them that trespass against us. And lead us not into temptation, but deliver us from evil.

Hail, Mary, full of grace, the Lord is with thee; blessed art thou among women, and blessed is the fruit of thy womb, Jesus. Holy Mary, sweet and loving queen of heaven, O mother of God, pray for us sinners, that we may see thee among the elect.

O Rex gloriae (Ascension)

O King of glory, Lord of hosts, who hast this day ascended in triumph above all the heavens, leave us not orphans; but send unto us the promise of the father, the spirit of truth, alleluia.

Angelus ad pastores ait (Christmas)

The angel said to the shepherds: I bring you tidings of great joy, for this day is born to you the saviour of the world, alleluia.

Hodie completi sunt (Pentecost)

Today were the days of Pentecost accomplished, alleluia; today the Holy Spirit appeared to the disciples in the form of fire, and gave them the gifts of grace: he sent them into the whole world to preach and bear witness: that he who shall believe and be baptized shall be saved, alleluia.

Haec est dies (Easter)

This is the day which the Lord hath made: let us rejoice and be glad in it, alleluia. I lay down and slept, and I rose up, for the Lord sustained me, alleluia.

Beati eritis

Blessed are you when men shall revile you, and persecute you, and speak all that is evil against you, falsely, for my sake. Be glad and rejoice, for your reward is very great in heaven.

O crux ave spes unica (Holy Week)

Hail, O cross, only hope, in this passiontide grant justice to the holy, and pardon to sinners.

Christe, adoramus te

O Christ, we adore thee and bless thee, for by thy holy cross thou hast redeemed the world. Lord, have mercy upon us.

Christe, adoramus te

G. C. Bianchi: Libro primo de motetti
(Venice, Magni, 1620)

Claudio Monteverdi
(1567-1643)

* F in source / *F in der Quelle*